PracticingLOVE

Reflective Times & Critical Thinking

RAYROSARIO

Revised Edition

Editor
Lu Herrera

Layout, Design, and Cover Art "In the Eyes of HOPE"
Ray Rosario

www.ray-rosario.com

DEDICATION

This book is dedicated to my parents & all those who have given and sacrificed their lives for the LOVE of Humanity.

CONTENTS

ACKNOWLEDGMENTS

To my entire family, domestic and abroad. They have loved and cared for me unconditionally. Milton and Jareslie both shaped me into the man I am today and taught me to LOVE them with all my being as my parents did for me. My friends whom have blessed me with support from the very beginning to build my foundation as an artist: Greg & Nelly, Ebby Antigua, Toby, Lu Herrera, Evelyn Soto, Betsy Vega, Insamo, Judge Sallie Manzanet-Daniels, Jennifer Zazo-Brown, Judge Dora Irizarry, Lucy Casanova Moreno, Jill Zdanow, Miriam Mora, Emily Vargas-Benedict, Nancy Graham, Michelle Danvers Foust, Disco Mike, Benny Casanova, Ms. Anonymous (who offered her intellect, guidance, and willingness to assist in the structuring of this book), and Victoria Donoghue. Alvaro for being a great artist, an inspiration, and friend. I'd also like to thank everyone else who assisted and supported me along the way. I wish I could list them all but that would be a book by itself. The Hasbun Family who adopted me and cared for me like a son during my college years. The Graham Family, Papa Graham provided my first studio where I discovered myself and became an artist. John Rivera, Luis T. Rodriguez Moctezume, and Jenny Vargas, with her wonderful heart, sponsored my second studio and other opportunities in conjuction with the future committees. Evelyn Duarte who believed in me and assisted with my first exhibit. Joe DelGreco for providing the amazing venue where I held my first exhibit. Erik Rucker who provided my third space so generously (twice). Alex Impagliazzo who became my first sponsor and patron; he purchased my first art work and became a great friend. Hydred Makabali who has inspired me since day one. She's an incredible woman who has challenged me in every way and has been a beacon of hope to me as well for many others. Google her and you will see why. Natasha Moradi, a key person in my transition to becoming an artist, has assisted me with spiritual guidance, knowledge, shared her poetry and allowed me to create from them. Her family who welcomed me into their home with kindness, generosity, and LOVE.

PREFACE

We are all creative beings on some levels. For some, it is creating images on canvas or using earthy materials such as clay, metal, and wood. For others, it's the art of storytelling. There is the composition of musical notes that move our senses or the free form movements of a dancer. Or, the architect who has the ability to transform landscapes into visual and livable wonders. These—and others—are all forms of art. I admire them all. Each one takes a skill; countless hours, days, months, and in some cases years of dedication to build an idea, and transform it into a work of artistic display. Each one affects the audience in a different way. As with any form of art, Practicing LOVE takes dedication and a willingness to learn how to tap into our inner power in order to uplift ourselves and share it with those around us in a positive manner.

As an artist, my artwork is an extension of who I am. Writing is a different medium for me. Usually when I reach for a graphite pencil, it's to start sketching my ideas. By that time, my creative process has already begun and has moved me in different directions. It's at that point when I am inspired to travel to the next phase of my creative journey. The first part being the formation of an idea. The rest of my creative process bridges that idea to my emotions, thoughts, beliefs, and life experiences. Rarely is the final outcome exactly as I originally sketched it. Life continuously affects my connection to color, space, composition, texture, tones, values, and lighting. The environment, the sounds around me, the time of day— whether it's day or night—contribute to the outcomes of my creations and inspirations. It's important for me to be present and grateful whenever possible.

I had stepped away from the corporate sector to dedicate my time to becoming an artist. I needed to understand what I was feeling and create the path to uncover my calling in life. I went against what most consider the norm and what I was taught to go after, a nine to five. I began an upward battle ever since, making my way in the unpredictable world of the arts. This is the hardest road I have ever followed but the most rewarding. The past and present started to form my work, formulated the way I thought and filled my body with life to produce. All exchanges became personal in the way I absorbed and internalized energies that deepened my connection to everything around me. It was as if life took off the blinders and opened the flood gates of transparency to the life I had not been living. A rebirth. There grew an excitement around new experiences. A different level of personal maturity evolved. I now had a new life to build with endless possibilities to create and form a destiny on my terms.

I was fortunate to have a father lay down a solid foundation of work ethics as my mother filled our home with unconditional love. The strength of a lasting, healthy two-parent household provided many life tools that have come in handy throughout my life. Maturing, I became keenly aware of the impact and value that combination would have on my identity and the life I had inherited. Through my parents, I learned to respect and honor all individuals, especially women. To love unconditionally. Love requires working out the hardest of problems by communicating honestly. We went through hard times but managed to work through them and remained a family unit. Learning to be honest with myself was the first step in my growth and being able to communicate my ideas and philosophy to others with the arts.

When I decided to become an artist, I didn't have any concrete plans. Although I knew that I would eventually need to sell my artwork in order to make a living, it wasn't about the money. It was about following my passion and listening to my internal voice. After two years of producing art, I felt ready to have my first exhibit. I researched galleries to understand the operational side. They required fifty to sixty percent of the selling price. I wasn't ready to give up so much of myself especially that early in my developing stages as an artist. I structured a plan for exhibits and created opportunities to expose my work. Soon I had my first exhibit, a second, and more. After a few, I realized that my art was starting to take on a life of its own. It was determining where I was going to exhibit, the work I was producing, the people I was meeting, and the new experiences that dictated the outcome of future work. The ongoing results of this journey have been amazing. I know this type of life isn't for everyone and it can be scary. I chose to run through fear rather than live with regret. I couldn't deny myself of living the way I felt inside. I also knew without great risk I would not see great results. I didn't know the right people. I didn't have the connections or mentors that would assist me on my journey. I understood that if I wasn't willing to push every bit of time, focus, and energy I had in my body towards my goals, passions, and dreams, then I would come up short. We have to feed our passions whatever they may be if we wish to see them flourish. This also holds true with all types of relationships as well.

I listened, observed, grew, and did the best I could to follow where the art would lead me. In time, my work intertwined with my sense of humanity. I volunteered doing art therapy with cancer-stricken children. One in particular was a nine-year-old girl named Carolina who had the strength and will to assist other kids despite her declining health. Through Carolina, I witnessed one person's undeniable courage, joy, and determination to fight for her life. She attended my first exhibit and a few others with the aid of crutches or a wheelchair. I dedicated each event to her. She gave more to me than I could have ever given her. She allowed me in her life with full transparency. Carolina left us at twelve years of age. I realized my life would encompass a lifetime of effort for the greater good and all its challenges. The way I internalized life changed because of my friendship with Carolina. The way she chose to face her life challenges adjusted my perspective as to how I should approach my personal challenges and obstacles. As a result, I created a painting, "Sunflower Bed," of her as a young woman making peace with her disease as she overlooks a bed of sunflowers located on the back cover of the book.

During this journey, I have and will continue to learn about myself as well as others. Engulfing my life with all forms of knowledge has become a way of life for me. I am simply sharing what I have learned and what has worked for me. The current climate within our society impelled me to share my principles, my ongoing process of Practicing LOVE. Social issues stemming from politics, racial division, social media-based identities, and the general disconnect we have with one another have shaped my way of being and outlook on life. I am not a writer, Guru or self-proclaimed anything. I'm just an artist sharing the many blessings that I have been privileged with witnessing and experiencing. I use different creative mediums to express myself. Sometimes, I create for my own need. A need that stems from an unexplained desire. At times, it's to expose my innermost emotions in a concrete form, an external extensions of my being. Mostly, it's due to what's happening in the global landscape and my personal exchanges with people. Practicing LOVE has elevated my awareness and grounded me with humility to become a better person. It has assisted in balancing my life and kept me grounded during trying times of hardship, uncertainty, and the changing conditions of our society. Balance in life is such a key factor to living and finding happiness.

If this book becomes instrumental to you in anyway, then this exercise was well worth it. If you wish to share your experience, please feel free and write to me at practicinglove1@gmail.com.

I thank you from the bottom of my heart for your support and love.

Always grateful,
ray

PRACTICING LOVE

We are at a critical time in history in which we are losing a vital connection to ourselves and humanity. Love is the grounding force that should be the basis of our thoughts, actions, and foundation.

Practicing LOVE is a universal framework to assist in developing and strengthening our capacity to love. It helps us work on increasing the love we have for ourselves while connecting with others in a healthy and positive manner. Practicing LOVE is an exercise that is based on performing acts of kindness—thoughtful gestures—that are done on a daily basis over the course of a year. This gives enough time for the mind to embed a consistent action into the subconscious and transform it into habitual behavior.

In the coming pages, I chose to address a few well-known topics that are critical to our development and growth process. Food for thought as they say. These issues often become obstacles that prevent us from loving to our full capacity.

Practicing LOVE will help us overcome some of these issues and keep balance in our lives. It takes more time for some than for others to work through life's challenges. This is why we should extend ourselves by Practicing LOVE.

Practicing LOVE is transparent and clear so all of humanity globally understands its actions becoming more powerful than words. This is a universal language and exercise. We must continue to evolve and enhance our lives. As a result, we will change the way we feel, see, and understand love. Our ability to give love freely will become a natural extension of ourselves.

INTRODUCTION

The idea for the Practicing LOVE book evolved from my time riding the NYC transit system. I witnessed the apathetic attitudes and the lack of common decency: the unhappy faces, rude treatment toward one another, forgetting common courtesies like offering a seat to those who need it, using profanity in front of children, and the list goes on and on. To be fair, it's not always like that. I do love my travel time. I utilize it productively. I read, formulate ideas, sketch, or plan my next projects. It can be pleasant, but as the city's population continues to grow so does the lack of patience shown by commuters.

Too many times I found myself caught up in other people's negative energies. I'd prepared myself to react aggressively in case a situation escalated rather than act with empathy and love to help de-escalate the situation so no one would be affected negatively. No matter how long or short of a time I was in transit, my mind was caught up in negative thoughts. I didn't like the way the environment was impacting my emotions and I wanted to minimize it. I spent many years working on grounding myself and becoming a better person prior to my commuting to the city. Even with all that work, I needed to fortify my inner resolve to operate and filter life through love under temperamental conditions beyond my control. Once I strengthened and built my love, I was able to change my thoughts and emotions through positive actions. In time, I was operating from a different frame of mind and consciousness. My actions and energy become second nature. Other areas of my life improved due to the change.

I'll share one experience I had while taking the train into Manhattan. I had been reading a book when a man got on the train at the 96th Street Station. He was angry and agitated, yelling and cursing. I couldn't tell if he was drunk, homeless, high—or suffered from mental issues. He entered the train on my left-hand side opposite of where I was sitting. He turned to his left and yelled, "Get the hell out of that seat" to a woman sitting in front of me. She raced out of the seat frightened but silent to the other side of the train. People from either side started to move away as he sat down. I place my items away slowly and prepared myself for an altercation in case he came at me to cause physical harm. I looked his way but not directly at him in order to keep an eye on him. He then yelled at me, "Move the hell over so I can sit there." I stayed calm as he came over and sat down without touching me. When he first entered cursing, I automatically started to assess his size, stability, and whether or not he was concealing a weapon. For a super split second, I thought of how best to do a UFC sleeping chokehold on this guy until help arrives. I'm not saying I would have been successful, but I had to be prepared to do something. Then I changed gears. I went into the frame of mind of Practicing LOVE, keeping my energy low and calm. I might have a chance to actually practice what I've gone over in my mind about these types of situations. I moved forward in my seat, turned my head slightly to face him, and gently addressed him: "I cannot allow you to cause harm to anyone on the train. I'm sorry but I cannot allow that to happen." The gentleman didn't say a word or look at me. Within a few seconds the train doors opened, he got up and left the train. He wasn't angry, didn't curse, just simply left. This could have turned out so many other ways but it didn't. I am not suggesting we confront others when in similar situations, especially since we don't know if the individual suffers from mental illness. I was fortunate the situation worked out this way. I placed my trust in faith and acted accordingly. I know the old me would have handled that very differently with nothing but testosterone. No bueno.

It took strength, maturity, and Practicing LOVE over time to work out things through love rather than a negative, emotional state of mind. Conflicts will always escalate for the worse if handled with mirrored aggression.

The more I put my thoughts about Practicing LOVE into action, the more I felt the need to share this exercise of empowering oneself with others. If this way of being assisted with what I considered to be my flaws, then it might help someone else.

We are all flawed and vulnerable no matter how much we work on ourselves. There is always room for improvement. Most of us are taught manners, courtesy, kindness, and respect. We are shown love growing up. The pressures of life tend to chew away at the core of what we have been taught as children. We react in a different manner when life's weight is on our shoulders, and we forget to put into practice what was taught. Our appearance starts to change in the eyes of those we cause hardship despite our physical attributes. We become what we feel inside. This is what is meant by "beauty is only skin deep." We need to correct this over time so we don't transform into destructive individuals harming ourselves and all those around us.

If we don't work a muscle, it loses its flexibility and strength. Practicing LOVE will keep that positive emotion "muscle" working so we can handle life's pressures from a solid place of strength, courage, and hope. When the mind is less distracted with negativity, our behavior and energy will reflect goodness and the power of love. Practicing LOVE is flexing that particular emotional muscle so we stay connected to our humanity.

There's space in the book for journal writing. Throughout the book I will suggest ways to use the journal as a way to assist in our journey. This book doesn't provide solutions to problems. Practicing LOVE is a long-term exercise, a stepping stone to improve our connection to humanity that will strengthen throughout our lifetime.

LOVE & OUR SURROUNDINGS

I view love as the greatest emotion we can ever feel within ourselves. Love is the keystone. Love is the strongest feeling necessary to survive and live with internal harmony that extends outward to all areas of our life. Love will make us excel, grow, and endure hardship. Love gives us the capacity to live past extreme measures and conditions. Love generates an authenticity that penetrates the spirit of others even if they are not familiar with it. Love opens up unlimited doors of opportunity and keeps us humble. Practicing LOVE is about the small steps that lead to the bigger changes in our lives.

We have entered an era of wanting more than we are giving, taking more than distributing, dismantling more than building, destroying more than loving. It is important to understand that we live in times where the political establishment is not on the side of the common people; for example, the middle class has nearly disappeared. Robert Reich who served under former presidents Gerald Ford and Jimmy Carter became Secretary of Labor from 1993 to 1997 under President Bill Clinton. He was also a member of President Barack Obama's economic transition advisory board. Mr. Reich is an insider who clearly understands the systems put in place. He disagrees with the injustice and off-balance of the economic structure and income inequality. He lectures, educates, and has written over 17 books informing us of the unfavorable systems the government and corporations have formed and the dangers of the disappearing middle class.

Future generations of graduates will drown in loans. It's very clear that the cost of education has expediently increased over the past few decades while the average household has held steady with minimal or no increase in salary wages. "Between 1993 and 2015, average tuition increased by 234%—when the inflation rate was just 63%. According to data from the Bureau of Labor Statistics, 46% of grads left college with debt in 1995, compared with 71% in 2015," reports Shana Lebowitz in the April 30, 2018, *Business Insider* article, "7 ways life is harder for millennials than it was for their parents." The system has crippled the students with debt delaying their contribution to our economy because they have no purchasing power not to mention the added emotional stress it creates.

The public school systems, depending on location, are set up for students to fail in society. We now value quantity rather than quality. Standardize testing has risen and it equates to memorization rather than learning. The system pushes students forward without fully understanding the curriculum. The number of diagnosed children with ADHD has risen along with the use of medications. I don't believe that is a coincidence. The government has shifted its resources and priority to the military and prison system rather than updating an antiquated public education system. Low socioeconomic areas get hit the worst.

There is false information being distributed through media outlets now labeled as fake news. Fake news is produced to manipulate the truth or spread fictional stories. It plays on our emotions so we react quickly, spreading information like wild fire. We should be aware of statements made by news media outlets stating "researchers say," "a study finds," or "experts declare." If we just do a little research, we will find more often than not the research/studies are funded by the companies that will benefit from the information being distributed. If we are not grounded or become critical thinkers, we become pawns in a bigger game where we become guinea pigs for pharmaceutical companies, storytellers for our government, product consumption addicts by manufacturers, financial slaves to corporate companies. Things are not going to get any easier before they get better. These situations will challenge and test our ability to love not only ourselves but also one another, to love those close to us as well as strangers and the world around us. Most important, it will test our hope and faith. We need to enhance the way we understand the true meaning of love in a society designed to strip it from our hearts.

Psychologists and philosophers have debated as to whether or not we are inherently selfish human beings. I believe, there are times when we need to be selfish and place ourselves before others. This is a positive form of self-love. We need to ensure that we are healthy in mind, body, and soul first. Without personal health we are incapable of truly helping others. Once we start to reach an emotionally healthy state, we can evolve to a higher emotional plane and make a difference in the lives of others. That is my focus.

Love will move and create change in every aspect of our life. We all have different meanings of love. Despite culture and language barriers, the universe will always respond to unify us in extreme situations and times. Love provides the freedom to extend our heart and compassion to others without expectations or reciprocity. When we give it with the pure intentions of our heart, it will return to us. The power of love is communicated through direct eye contact and action. The words we deliver hold no weight on their own without the supportive actions needed to build a foundation of trust and honor.

Love is not generated by physical actions alone. The emotions and energy tied to our actions make it valid. This is known as internal intent. Internal intent is our energy life force that individuals feel when we have an exchange. If our actions differ from our intent, others may sense it and question the purpose of the exchange. Some are able to detect the situation and not accept it, or act in the manner we were not expecting because deceit was detected in our actions and energy. Others may not detect it. More often than not the end result will not be successful. This applies to all areas of our life. If our internal intent is pure of heart, there are no regrets with the end results. If someone gives up a seat on the subway to a pregnant woman because s/he was told to do it, it's not the same as performing the act because one truly wishes to do it.

The joy of being able to take any action and feel the blessings behind it will create balance for us as well as the receiver's life. It's a cycle that needs to be practiced and passed onto future generations. This is a real possibility. We need to place true faith behind it to see it work. Our strength will grow when we continue to practice and allow these gestures of kindness to evolve. These small steps will empower us to take our place in life by living and setting an amazing example. We hold the key and power of our destiny if we choose. We may be frightened to find some of the answers during our soul searching. The beautiful aspect of this is that we can start to change at any time on our own or with the help of others. The effort we place into this exercise will determine our personal truth and outcome.

TOUCHING BASE WITH THE PAST

There are a few main sources that plant the seeds of pain in our hearts: family upbringing, environment, past relationships, etc. Sometimes people move through various types of relationships like a revolving door. People have difficulty understanding how love works due to the many hardships they have encountered. We need to learn how to recognize the issues causing us pain, tend to them, and heal to keep them from shaping the rest of our lives and relationships.

Family Upbringing. Love can be determined by the way it's given to us by our primary caregivers as we are growing up. Human contact and love is our innate way of being. Without it we lose part of our human experience to exchange energies, grow, and develop from them, especially if the main ingredient, love, is not present. Many children who have not had ample physical and emotional attention are at higher risk for behavioral, emotional and social problems as they grow up. "The critical role of social touch throughout the lifespan is considered, with special attention to infancy and young childhood, a time during which social touch and its neural, behavioral, and physiological contingencies contribute to reinforcement-based learning and impact a variety of developmental trajectories," writes Carissa J. Cascio in *Developmental Cognitive Neuroscience* (2018). In addition to the cognitive benefits, contact by touch transfers the parent's energy to the infant reinforcing safety, protection, caring, and the building blocks of maternal love.

As adults, we believe we are freely choosing our partner at will because of our intuition and the ideology of romanticism. In reality, that could be far from the truth if we understand our past. A family that displays misguided love through physical and emotional abuse alters the reality of love. Because of such upbringings, an individual will seek abusive relationships or create turmoil because it is equated with misguided love. As children, we are not responsible for the hardships of our upbringing. As adults, we must take responsibility, learn to deal with our turmoil, and do our best to break the cycle of abuse in order to ensure we build better lives for ourselves. We should not pass it on or have others be victims of our circumstances. We tend to respond with blame, attack, try and hold others accountable, and believe they need to fix our situations for us. No one can fix or generate our healing other than ourselves.

Environment. Once we understand that our surrounding is harming our spirit to love, we must build our strength and courage to change it. If we don't, we will become that which we fought so hard against to survive. The history of human survival has shown that no matter how difficult our circumstances, the will to LOVE life has always triumphed.

Author/Journalist Martha Gellhorn has experienced many wars firsthand starting with the Spanish Civil War in 1937. She became a bearing witness and wrote in wonder and amazement about the Barcelonians who during the months of bombings still gathered in the opera house to perform for their countrymen. The singers being thin due to the lack of food still sang. There were no rehearsals in this time of war so the singers used song sheets. This occurred as family, friends, and neighbors became casualties of war. We will formulate any and all means of survival tactics to overcome death and hardship under the most extreme situations.

The arts became an instrument vital to human survival. Music affects the brain and has the power to change mood and behavior. It relaxes or excites crowds. Music and the arts assist in the healing and therapy of recovering patients, such as those dealing with depression and Parkinson's. The arts require no deciphering translation of language. It overrides cultural and generational barriers to ensure a personal journey into oneself connecting what we internalize to visuals.

The arts ignite our senses while keeping our vulnerability hidden from the public if we choose. The arts demand our presence. It's one of the few times we are engaged and present in the moment with all our senses working simultaneously ensuring we are connected to each other and the world.

Along my journey I was asked to create a workshop for an organization's staff retreat and decided to do it based on the theme of environment. This was an exercise to show how the environment impacts one's consciousness and behavior. I placed a long horizontal sheet of paper along the wall where everyone could pick a spot and create images based on my instructions. I had everyone lie down, close their eyes, and go into a relax state of mind as I played soft music for 10 to 15 minutes. I directed them to envision a safe place. Afterwards I asked them to draw their mental trip on the paper with crayons. Most of the results were sketches of beaches, suns, palm trees, and nature. Two individuals drew pictures with people in them but most had drawn themselves alone even those who were married or in relationships. When asked, they informed me that they didn't have enough alone time. The two that drew additional people with them did have enough alone time.

Next I asked them to position themselves in their original places for the second part of this exercise. I started with the same relaxed music except I didn't give any instructions, assuming they would naturally conjure up the same safe haven due to the music. As time elapsed, the intensity and structure of the music gradually changed until it became intense, loud, and chaotic. I threw items across the room and slammed things on the floor. Once I stopped, I asked them to draw the images they experienced on a clean sheet of paper. Most sketches were abstract. Some of the images had erotic lines or displayed violence. The colors they chose were hard reds and darker colors with hard-pressed lines compared to the first that contained lighter colors and softer lines. They fidgeted around while creating the second as opposed to the first time when their body postures were more relaxed.

Once I got them settled, I sat them down in front of their sketches so they can compare the difference between the two. They were able to see how the changes in the environment altered the outcome of their emotions and vision. One even realized that they needed to move from their neighborhood to improve their outcome. I explained the association of color with feelings and the impact it has on the subconscious. Whether we understand this or not, we develop an internal language relating messages with colors that bonds us in many forms such as actions we take against each other (ex. gang colors). Wearing reds, in fashion or make up, attracts attention. Wearing black can be a sign of sophistication or death. The blues, yellows and light purples triggers happiness and cheer. Several informed me they had dark colors in their living spaces because it was their favorite or it was associated with their culture. We are impacted by the nature of our environment both internally and externally. We have to rethink the colors of our apartments and homes. We need to choose more tranquil colors to help the mind and spirit settle down once we arrive home to help with balance.

Past relationships. There is always something to learn about others and ourselves from every relationship. An unfavorable past will try to dictate our present experiences and potential opportunities if we are not aware of it. We need to work and get past the pain, ask the right questions, and reflect to better understand what occurred and why. Reflection is a major component for growth and forward momentum in all areas of our lives. It will allow us to forgive. Forgiveness of ourselves and of others is one of the key elements to grow past the hardship to better ourselves. It's quite difficult almost impossible to move forward without it. Forgiveness requires time, patience, and the willingness to let go and grow. It's one of the hardest things to come to terms with. Forgiveness comes when we have taken the time to digest the situation from all angles with a clear head and formulate a healthy approach to resolve the situation that doesn't involve anger, resentment, hostility, or bitterness. We are then able to become the bigger person to resolve our conflict and forgive so our hearts, mind, and soul can start to grow and heal. Forgiveness is not condoning a person's action or forgetting it but allowing all parties to move forward with a clean slate. This takes work. It's not keeping the past situation in a prison file ready to open at a moment's notice to attack and prevent all parties from entering the healing process. If we commit to forgiveness, there is no record whether the individual stays in our lives or not. Forgiveness allows us to be free from emotional bondage and become truly compassionate individuals.

Romantically, we can and will mask our hearts thinking we are healed and jump into another relationship. Once our new courting partner behaves or says something that causes us to be uncomfortable, it can trigger a flashback—a feeling attached to the past. Our past emotions take over. Anger and fear dictate our actions instead of love. Those emotions are projected onto the new relationship. We will lose sight on how to resolve matters rationally.

It is imperative that we work on ourselves and have an open mind to growing on all levels. Unless we are willing to work on it, we cannot expect our new insights or awareness to lead to behavior change. Let's first heal and take care of ourselves before we decide to share our lives with others. We need to extend our love not try and find it in others.

HONESTY

We have to remain honest with ourselves. This is not about passing or failing, judging or categorizing, being good or behaving badly. It's about opening up to another level of consciousness for growth, one where we can generate pure love and give it freely.

The success of this exercise relies on being honest with ourselves. If we ignore areas of our life where we are having problems and bury them, we will never heal. That's the truth. Honesty is knowing that we are imperfect. It's part of human nature. We all have imperfections in the eyes of another. We shouldn't feel ashamed, embarrassed, or humiliated nor should we allow others to use these words against us as weapons to suppress us. It takes courage and strength to admit our imperfections. The ego will blind us to this reality and have us living in a mirage that hinders our growth. Accepting this piece of information as truth will go a long way and assist us in creating a healthy state of mind and processing ourselves and others in a positive manner.

This is another opportunity to use the journal portion of the book. You may wish to write it down in order to figure out how best to work on them. Seeing it on paper is a reminder of what needs to be addressed and helps reinforce a forward momentum to healing. We tackle them one at a time and make amends—to ourselves or to others. In time the list will decrease and even disappear, leaving us with a great foundation to start re-building ourselves for a brighter future. When we generate this love, other areas of our life will start to improve and change automatically.

The strength and power of Practicing LOVE with others comes as a result of us practicing it with ourselves first. In the beginning before I started to produce art, I felt the need to understand what was driving my life in this direction. What was I feeling inside to choose the path of becoming an artist? What's the purpose? What am I going to do with this? I understood that being in relationships, continuing the same life patterns with the same unhealthy choices would keep me from discovering the answers. I needed to love myself enough to make changes.

One of the ways I chose to practice caring for my Self was through celibacy. I was celibate for a few years. I needed to be selfish with my love for my Self. It elevated my consciousness and it was an effective way for me to find answers. It allowed me to grow, gave me clarity, and built my inner strength. It took away distractions and detours that didn't pertain to my personal growth goals. It's as if I climbed out of the swimming pool and stood on the edge overlooking this overcrowded, congested pool, and I couldn't tell the difference from one person to another. No room to move or inhale clear air that would fill my lungs with vibrant life. I never knew or envisioned this because I was engulfed in the environment. My life and behavior towards everything changed. I understood the importance of being present in the moment. I was grateful and thankful and made sure those who contributed to my life knew it and felt it. I became restructured and refocused. It brought a sense of calmness because I was now more grounded than ever. I also understood that I was evolving into a higher state of spiritual consciousness. Some close to me thought I was a bit extreme, but this was a necessity for my growth. I started to make other changes like engaging in different knowledge-based activities that added value, growth, and allowed continuous happiness including nature, soirees, and fitness. All the elements that balanced my life with harmony and a sense of purpose. I needed to separate myself from everything, both physically and emotionally. I have never stepped back into the person I was prior to practicing celibacy nor would I wish to because of how much my life has been enriched. It took time before I was ready to give to others again. Once I felt rooted, I was then able to start Practicing LOVE with others. To do so, I needed to start with myself. For anyone reading this book (especially men), if you truly wish to change the way you see life and reach a different level of awareness, try celibacy—even for the short term. Focus on yourself and the internal goals you wish to achieve. Things will fall into place and you'll be surprised at the amazing outcome.

Achievements fulfill us and drive us to become better in all we do. Setting goals and obtaining them is the natural process of success as an active participant in life. Achieving personal and career happiness should be part of our goals. If our motives are to disguise our internal unhappiness by hunting for a new job, moving to a new location, finding a new partner, buying a new car, or going on a shopping spree for clothing—that sense of glee will provide only a modicum of satisfaction. Each is an external solution for healing a deeper internal wound.

The increase of unhappy individuals in the U.S. is peaking like no other time in our past and so is the spending. Personally, I've heard people mention numerous times that they are going shopping to make them feel better and release some stress. Food for thought about two topics as an example: U.S. commerce systems are in place to create such an atmosphere to drive health and the psyche of the population to seek and sort out quick fix solutions. Create a problem and sell the solution. Let's take food for example. We know that GMO's and processed foods are the cause for many health issues and obesity in this country. Quick fix: diet pills, gadgets, and saran wrap that you can wrap around your waist that require minimal or no effort to see results for weight loss and tons of medication and therapy for mental health issues.

Even within this self-help book, we need to consider the source. There are great writers, advertising giants, and companies who benefit financially from our unhappiness by creating products that falsify needs for our life experiences. Melanie Lindner writes article in *Forbes* January 15, 2009, issue: "Americans spent $11 billion in 2008 on self-improvement books, CDs, seminars, coaching and stress-management programs—13.6% more than they did back in 2005, according to Market data Enterprises, an independent Tampa-based research firm that tracks everything from adoption agencies to funeral homes. Latest forecast: 6.2% annual growth through 2012.

Infomercials—peddling everything from weight-loss programs to quick-and-easy real estate schemes--pulled in $1.4 billion in 2008, down 5% from 2007 but still the largest by sales volume of any self-help medium. The hot growth area--up nearly 11% in the last year, to $527 million--includes holistic institutes."

There really are no quick fix remedies to the problems mentioned. We have to educate and arm ourselves. With time and effort we will have the proper solutions assisting us in our journey to better our health and mental state of mind. Practicing LOVE is a long-term exercise that assists with healing from the deepest part of the wound not the surface with a quick fix as we remain honest with ourselves.

INSECURITIES

Being honest helps us face another common disease that stunts our growth, ability to trust, and inhale the love of one another in every capacity. There are many levels of insecurities. Some of us are great at disguising them. No more than clothing hiding our insecurities about our body and our skin hiding our internal ones. They are multi-layered. Each one is different according to the individual. The one I will be referring to is the most common to couples.

In Alain de Botton's, *The Art of Therapy*, he writes: "Love is meant to be a pleasurable part of life, yet there are no people we are more likely to hurt, or to be hurt by, than those we are in a relationship with. The degree of cruelty that goes on between lovers puts established enemies to shame. We hope the love will be a powerful source of fulfillment, but it sometimes turns into an area for neglect, unrequited longing, vindictiveness, and abandonment. We become sullen or petty, nagging or furious, and without quite grasping how or why, destroy our lives and those we once claimed to care for."

Insecurities are a natural part of life. Everyone develops them due to experiences, peer pressure, the media, etc. We should not allow them to define us or dictate the structure of our lives. Insecurities are like weeds growing in a beautiful lush garden. If we don't treat our insecurities, they will outgrow and infect the beauty that exists within us. It will spread from one area of our lives to another.

The depth of those insecurities and the amount of time we deal with them is up to us. Life will test us on all levels, especially when it comes to our capacity for introspection. That ability to search deep inside of ourselves to figure out who we are as individuals. Life does this to build us up, educate us, and give us a deeper understanding of the work needed to strengthen our foundation with our own truth, to lessen the capacity to stray. It will allow us to understand how to listen to our instincts and understand why we exist as individuals.

If we cannot trust because of past experiences, then we believe we do not deserve the best the next experience has to offer with love. Deserving the best is our choice and we should never settle. We have to allow it to enter our lives and accept it in order to move forward. We often let our past determine the outcome of our future. We do this by never taking the proper time to heal.

We have to be able to see our personal value and love ourselves enough to heal and grow. This freedom will allow us to encounter new relationships with awe. This level of happiness does exist. We tend to settle because we need to find instant gratification instead of taking the time to reflect, understand our actions and reactions, and stop blaming others. If we are in a healthy relationship and acknowledge this in time, our willing partner will stand by us and support all that we do. This will build a solid foundation of trust and love in the relationship. If we do not acknowledge it, we will destroy our partner and every chance of ever finding it with that person and experiencing love in its pure form, if that is your intent. We are in place to empower our partner, not hinder them. Our insecurities and fears become another person's limitations.

It is easier to settle than work on facing our fears. We then choose partners that are less threatening to our insecurities, partners that will not challenge us to fix or face our fears. We settle and never live life to its fullest potential. In time, we feel contempt. Love doesn't truly bond such a relationship. A false sense of security allows us to live with our insecurities, because we surround ourselves with everything that will keep them suppressed.

We can willingly decide to encapsulate ourselves in a cage due to the fear of being hurt. Insecurities will have us chasing someone who is not supportive of us. They just reinforce our weaknesses to keep us in our cage, a cage that we built ourselves or allow others to structure for us. This may occur because we happen to be weak or inexperienced with life at the time. Not healing and jumping from one relationship to another will keep us in a clouded state and allow us to keep leaving a trail of victims.

The mind is so powerful that it can create scenarios that did not exist; passing it for reality and causing problems and issues, creating distance and space in the relationship. This combination will keep us in a safe place while keeping others at arm's length never allowing anyone close enough to cause hurt or grow as a couple/individual. The more friction in a relationship, the safer we will feel. Insecurities will have us control all those feelings that are connected to our emotions while keeping our vulnerability at bay. For some of us, this is the only way we know how to love and be loved. Vulnerability becomes the enemy.

In truth, vulnerability is the key to experiencing love in its true form. It will allow us to grow beyond measure and achieve personal greatness. Vulnerability can be very frightening. Who wishes to subject themselves to hurt? Vulnerability allows us to grow in every aspect. It allows us to reach out for help when we are at our lowest and in our darkest hour. We can be vulnerable without fear of being hurt or being taken advantage of. Becoming grounded and working on ourselves by Practicing LOVE will assist in taking down our walls. We can better connect with the true individuals that we are. Some of us men seem to have trouble in this area. We tend to think it makes us look weak, not a manly thing to do. It takes strength to be sensitive. It is about understanding and being strong enough to empathize with situations and support our women. Our pride and ego need to be tamed and adjusted so we can evolve past these stigmas. It will then allow vulnerability and sensitivity to complete us, not hinder us.

By reflecting, we will gain the experience of hardship and start to look at gains instead of the losses. We gain the knowledge of having a better vision of ourselves as well as what we would like in our lives. We will be able to see other's true colors before investing a major part of our lives and heart. Reflecting will allow us to see the signs and red flags before we are in too deep. It will then allow us to make an intelligent choice about continuing the relationship and how to proceed. We always have a choice. Fear and the lack of faith will take that choice away from us. We surrender our strength and power to create change for ourselves and others when we lose hope. It's about arming ourselves with information to make the proper decision.

There are times when we date someone who is unaware of how deep his/her insecurities lie or have not yet healed from a previous relationship. We can only assist and be supportive when those insecurities start to arise and affect the relationship. If they make little or no effort to address the issue for themselves, then there is nothing we can do. From that point on, we are allowing our partner's projected insecurities to cause us harm. In return, we can become protective of ourselves. This cycle can start to cause both our partner and ourselves harm. Loving someone means being strong enough to let them go if we are causing them harm and are unable to heal or work on ourselves. The more we hold on, the more irreparable damage we are causing. We need to move forward in our healing process. If we love someone on any level, then our actions are the outcome of how can we enhance their lives not take from them with selfish acts or intentions. Not all relationships are meant to lead into marriage, even if that is our intension. When we keep an open mind and process life through a filter of love, we will gain all the benefits life has to offer. Loving someone is a responsibility, not acts of recklessness created by selfishness. Some of us tend to think that love is about what I can get out of this individual or situation rather than what can I give or contribute.

Healing requires quiet time without putting up all the safeguards of distractions to avoid dealing with the true issue. Quiet time is about traveling into the reflective solitude state with your thoughts in order to process the previous relationship(s) and move forward. This is quite difficult to obtain at first. Big city minds have been programed to work non-stop. We may give up at our first attempts to silence the mind but eventually we will be able to accomplish it. We have to find a space or create the environment, if possible, to achieve this state of mind. I'm not referring to a super elevated place of Zen or lighting enough candles to burn down city blocks. Just making the time and finding a place that reduces distraction near to nothing will work. One of the easiest places to connect and reflect is in nature. It is crucial to our mental health that we make time to reflect.

We can begin to process and think about our contributions to the relationship, re-adjusting so we can prevent them from future occurrences. Writing a list of our strengths and weaknesses when it comes to communicating in a relationship will allow us to build upon our weak areas in order to move forward in a positive direction. Recycled love without reflection and healing creates sleepwalkers with hollow hearts leaving a trail of victims reversing the role and becoming a victimizer.

Time and reflection will heal our wounds so we can see a clear picture of how we envision our lives and with whom. We then start to build and achieve personal happiness. With enough time and healing, we will be ready to engage in other relationships, both romantically and with friendships. We owe it to ourselves. Then will we be capable of passing these life lessons down to children, family, and friends. When we do decide to have exchanges, we are sharing and giving our personal happiness.

Sometimes it requires professional assistance, someone who is trained and can view the situation from an objective point of view. If we are not able to deal with the healing process ourselves, it is essential to get professional assistance.

We have all felt some level of insecurity at one time or another, big or small. At times we create a false illusion thinking that we are going to get into a perfect relationship without bumps and hurdles. Being secure allows for disagreements and hardships to occur without us running for the hills or leaving skid marks at the first sign of trouble. Surviving the hard times paves the road for a greater future together. It allows for us to process life and information from a healthy state of mind. We are able to figure out the source causing the insecurity, think it through, resolve it or bring it under containment. Not spiral down a rabbit hole without an exit.

Being in a relationship shouldn't mean encasement, it should represent freedom. Freedom to grow with our partner as well as individuals. That's a three-part component. It allows for trust to bond the love between the two not fear. Loving someone requires work for progression. The healthier we are internally before we enter a relationship, the less work is required. It leaves more time to enjoy each other's love and build a strong foundation. We have to cultivate the relationship. This expands our level of communication so that we can understand each other through direct eye contact and energy at times with no words. It keeps the balance. It allows us to be strong and supportive when our partner needs us. In return they will reciprocate.

Being secure and in a healthy state of mind allows us to understand the difference of loving someone and being in love with them. It provides the room and space for our love to mature on other levels so we can share our greatness. The benefits of being secure are many.

If all goes well, insecurities will be a thing of the past. Similar feelings may arise in the future. By that time, we will be well equipped to handle them so they don't cause us, family, friends, or partner harm and become uncontrollable weeds in a beautiful garden.

FEAR

I had to overcome my shyness of treading into unknown territory. I risked everything to become an artist. At some point, I understood I had nothing to lose. I was starting from scratch. I had people around me who loved me but couldn't support what they couldn't see or understand. I knew what I felt inside was real even though I had nothing concrete to show for it. There were those close to me who doubted and even made fun of me behind my back. It was hurtful only because these were childhood friends. This occurred when I chose to change my life and follow my dreams to become an artist. I also refused to give others any power over my life and destiny. I couldn't be angry for long after processing and understanding their actions. I knew it would take time and once I started to manifest my visions, they would understand. As I became successful, others started to support me. They saw and felt my motivation and dedication. People will assist and doors will open once they see that you are vested and believe in yourself. Cliché as it may sound if you don't believe in yourself, no one else will. I learned to create my own opportunities when doors weren't open. In time, I surrounded myself with individuals more successful and knowledgeable than I in any field of profession I could find. I drew off their energy, intellect, life, and drive. Over the years, I still remained close to certain friends. Interestingly enough, those who didn't support my ambitions faded away. We were moving in very different directions. Some of those friends decided they didn't wish to continue our friendship because it evolved into something different than they knew. That's a personal choice. I also had to let go of friends who were takers. No fault of their own. That's just how people are sometimes. I didn't have any more to give and I was being drained. There was nothing replenishing the relationship. I will always have love for them, but I needed to move forward. It didn't change the way I felt. If they need me, I will still be there for them. They helped me become the man that I am today. I am grateful.

We should be true to ourselves and not be afraid of losing or separating from relationships. Individuals will come in and out of our lives for short or extended periods of time and for many reasons and lessons. Being present without motives will allow us to see these reasons and lessons if we are in a healthy and willing state of mind. The lessons we need to learn for growth will keep repeating itself until we are ready to receive it so we can grow into the next stage in our journey.

Part of this growth allowed me to understand and see that others would try to impose their own fears onto me. I heard what they had to say, but it really had nothing to do with me. I have difficulty understanding why others might consciously encage themselves in believing they couldn't achieve goals or dreams. Hearing the number of times others place limitations upon themselves made me realize many live with a false sense of security. Security based on fear. Control is an illusion that we generate in order to feel safe in the world and cope with the evil that surrounds us. It's a survival mechanism. It allows us to move forward with limitations if processed incorrectly.

Some people think they are actually guaranteed to arrive home every day when they step outside their doors. That their lives are exempt from death. If we simply understand that life's security doesn't exist and we are not guaranteed life every day, then there is nothing we can't achieve within our lifetime. Even being home is not a living guarantee. A storm can wipe out our home. A neighbor can accidentally have a fire and destroy everything we own and even take our lives. We see these scenarios almost every day on the news. Still, we think we are invincible and death will not come knocking at our door.

When we are unfamiliar or uncomfortable or fearful on any level, we will do the only thing that comes natural and that is to protect ourselves and form a wall. Sometimes we do this even before any situation has arisen. This wall keeps all elements at bay but also imprisons us from any growth.

Fear is at the core of all that prevents us from living an amazing and fruitful life. Some of these limitations are self-induced. Tasting life without fear will take a lifetime to fill it with all we wish and desire. We hold the key to manifest all that our minds conceptualize. Others live vicariously because of fear; it turns into anger, resentment, jealousy, and any other word we can think of that is harmful. We spiral down into negativity, instead of using that energy to propel us forward. No one is placed above another. Self-placement empowers movement in the subconscious and leads us to think we are less valuable or unequal when in fact we are all the same and the dream is ours if we wish to live it.

Most successes are built on failures, roadblocks, challenges, struggles, setbacks, and obstacles; all are designed to strength our weaknesses and build long-term successes. We tend to fear these words and look at them negatively instead of in a positive manner. These are the learning experiences that are going to guide us up the right paths, both from a professional and personal perspective. Once we have learned and evolved, they become tools so we can educate others following in the same footsteps. The integrity of our success depends on extending ourselves to others with pure intentions of paying it forward. It is our duty and responsibility to share our knowledge with kindness and love whenever possible.

I learned that the word failure is not failing unless you have given up one hundred percent without ever trying again to achieve what you set out to do in the first place.

One of the few things I understood about the excuses surrounding failure is that is wasn't the right time, right opportunity, right person, or circumstances needed to achieve what one set out to do and be successful. I never failed. I just found a different way of achieving my goals. This will always be the case if you never give up and are persistent with patience. That is why it is vital and important to build and have patience, so we can then see the right opportunities when they arrive without settling. We have to be prepared to walk away from an opportunity or situation if it conflicts with our values and morals. Even if we can see, smell, and taste how close we are to what we wish to obtain. Success will come with all the right elements in place to sustain our dreams long term. Not short term for instant gratification by giving up what we believe in. We determine what the meaning of success is for ourselves, not others or society.

Everyone's definition of success is different. Examples can range from owning a home to renting in a better neighborhood. Having an ice cream truck business to building a multimillion-dollar company. Having a stressless job to pulling-out-your-hair-by-the-end-of-the-day-job. We all have a different way of looking at life and not everyone determines success by finances. Many people are financially successful and unhappy with life.

Practicing LOVE will help us overcome many obstacles to create amazing results. Fear will never have a grip on us in the same way. In some cases, it will never return or not in the same capacity where it will hinder us from achieving our version of greatness. Fear transforms into a precautionary measuring tool we use to assure we take and make the right decisions regarding our next steps in life.

Overcoming fear has led to some of the greatest movements of our time. Examples of the power of love through unification—before the Internet—occurred during the countercultural social movements that developed in the 60's. The strength and power of love united millions for common causes that sparked a change in regulations across the country from civil rights, woman's liberation, anti-war, gay rights to the Hispanic and Chicano movements. Most of these movements were based on non-violent actions and demonstrations. Love for a greater good of humanity peaked like no time before. Sometimes we are called to love others with our entire being that we choose to give up our lives for it. Most of us recognize names like Mother Teresa, Mahatma Gandhi, and Martin Luther King Jr. There are others like Rachel Corrie, Daniel Ellsberg, Gary Webb, Mark Lombardi, The Mirabal Sisters, and Edward Snowden among others who embraced death, imprisonment, and exile due to LOVE for humanity. Love achieves what most consider impossible. In recent years we have been able to unite and protest against issues that affected the majority, but we are not emotionally strong enough to protest with boycotts against products, services, and with the mighty dollar or the vote. Financial boycotts are a game changer, but we need to be stronger, grounded, and operate from a pure place of love valuing our worth in order for this to work. We have seen racially motivated advertisements. We uncover clothing lines that are manufactured in overseas sweatshops by children and adults who work endless hours in dangerous environments with inhumane treatment and being paid close to nothing. We witness industrial companies polluting and destroying our environment. Yet every two weeks, we can't wait to spend our hard earned money on their clothing and products. We witness industrial companies polluting and destroying our environment. Yet every two weeks, we can't wait to spend our hard earned money on their clothing and products. We have now become product consumption addicts fixated on name brands and the latest trends. We consume with the mindset that we are financial sound and successful even when we are not. This is a major reason why the average American household does not have a savings account, lives paycheck to paycheck, and lacks the discipline to save for a rainy day. Maurie Backman wrote an article for *USA Today* stating that "40 percent of U.S. adults don't have enough savings to cover a mere $400 emergency. Given the number of U.S. adults who couldn't come up with $400 at a moment's notice, it's encouraging to see that the average savings account balance is upward of $16,000. Furthermore, that figure refers only to savings accounts, which means that those with checking accounts, money market accounts, and CDs could be sitting on far more cash than that. That $16,420, to be clear, also doesn't factor in retirement savings. Still, that number starts to look less rosy when we dig a little deeper. While the average U.S. savings account contains $16,420, the median savings account balance across American households is $4,830. And when you have a median that's considerably lower than the average, it means that most people have less than the average." We need to change these statics and our consumption rate. We need to place value on savings. It's clear that all households aren't able to accomplish this due different circumstances, but we have to make every effort to break this cycle so we and our future children will not fall prey to financial hardship.

The financial effects on federal workers during the 35 days of the longest U.S. federal government shutdown (December 22, 2018 to January 25, 2019) provides a valuable lesson. Eight hundred thousand workers were affected. Many federal workers and their families couldn't make rent or mortgage payments and missed bills. A large percentage of workers collected unemployment and sought assistance from food banks. One federal prison guard in Louisiana attempted suicide after posting his financial hardships on Facebook. One would think they would be in a better financial position considering their wages and benefits. These are all major reasons why establishing a type of savings account is vital. It is imperative to start savings as soon as possible. We need to prepare as best we can for future, unforeseen emergencies short or long term if we are able to survive such matters.

We have an uphill battle in front of us. Our strength doesn't come from fighting all the battles (humanitarian causes). It comes when we choose one and fight with all our heart and might. The results will come and surpass our expectations. These are not just battles to fight oppression, wages, safety, and equality. There is a different war occurring. A spiritual war has manifested and now we have to fight to save our souls for the greater good of humanity. This is an internal battle to win the external war.

History has shown us that unification is considered a weapon in the eyes of the elites and those within the government working for them. A closer look at our current status and you can clearly see much separation has been formulated to keep the majority angry and weak. Something those with evil agendas weren't able to do as affectively before the Internet, commercialism, and reality TV shows. This keeps us from organizing to the next level after protesting. As long as we fight among ourselves, we will not be focused and remain suppressed.

In Martin Luther King Jr.'s first book *Stride Towards Freedom* about the Montgomery bus boycott, he wrote: "The phrase 'passive resistance' often gives the false impression that this a sort of 'do-nothing method' in which the resister quietly and passively accepts evil. But nothing is further than the truth. The method is passive physically, but strongly active spiritually." He also states about nonviolence "...that it does not seek to defeat or humiliate the opponent, but to win his friendship and understanding. The aftermath of nonviolence is the creation of the beloved community, while the aftermath of violence is tragic bitterness." Another characteristic of understanding the power of love that reaches far beyond the boycott is to understand the root and source of people's actions. He writes, "...the attack is directed against forces of evil rather than against persons who happen to be doing the evil. It is evil that the nonviolence resister seeks to defeat, not the persons victimized by evil." This applies to many aspects of our lives. These and others writings of love from our past humanitarians need to continue to be resurrected so that we can build our future with great core values.

A prime example of the power of forgiveness and Martin Luther King Jr.'s point on the forces of evil occurred in Cleveland, Ohio, where Robert Godwin, a 74-year-old man, was shot to death as he was walking home from Easter dinner by Steve Stephens, 37. Mr. Godwin was survived by two daughters, Debbie Godwin and Tonya Godwin-Baines. Both mention in an interview by Anderson Cooper (CNN) that they forgave Mr. Stephens and grieved for his parents. They both credit their father for teaching them about faith and forgiveness. Tonya added, "It's just what our parents taught us. They didn't talk it, they lived it. Neighbors would do things to us and we would say, 'Dad, are we going to forgive them? Really?' And he would say, 'Yes, we have to." The Godwin family understood evil dictated the actions of Steve. They chose to live in faith and demonstrate the power of forgiveness. We truly have to live by example so our future generations may rise above extreme situations and operate from a home of love in their hearts, not hate or fear.

THE VOID & DISCONNECT EFFECTS

We are living through unprecedented times where we need to have a clear understanding of our personal truth. We are exposed to an increasing amount of duplicitous information and more events commingled with extreme images of life and death, beauty and violence. So much so that we have created within ourselves a higher tolerance for it—and we have disengaged even further from our emotions in order to deal with this influx of information and images. We created a void in our psyche as a place to retreat, one of safety and neutrality. Thereby creating a disconnection with any emotion that can cause any hurt, pain, or even love. Our connection with empathy is losing the battle. This void didn't exist to this capacity prior to the existence of the World Wide Web and social media platforms. Before the Internet, kids and teenagers had each other to develop friendships. Now they compete for it with the world on social media platforms.

Since its inception, the Internet has provided many benefits and even wealth for people. We are more connected than ever as a global society. We are able learn and see what's going on around the world in real time. We can develop both business and personal relationships on an international level. We can support and assist many on a global scale. Thanks to certain social media platforms we know what's happening with family and friends (and strangers) without speaking to them because everything is posted from meals to bathroom habits, vacations to break ups. It's the norm for Internet behavior. It has also changed the way we communicate and get to know each other. It has given courage to those who are introverts while weakening face-to-face communication. The latter gives us Internet courage. With no face-to-face exchange, we feel there is nothing to lose. We never met in person, shook hands and touched, made eye contact when conversing, or absorbed each other's scent. Without personal exchanges of energies there is nothing to remember or hold on to. There is no human development that connects us emotionally with someone else. There is no thought to ending communication with an individual (ghosting) with the blink of an eye. We are losing a basic human function: common courtesy. No reasons, no explanations that allow for personal growth on either sides.

Think of the impact technological advances has on society. These multi-media diversions blur the lines of reality. We are meant to believe social media creates a cyber-community to keep us close; however, it actually creates a gap between us; it's a detachment that keeps us apart from one another. That's the strength and illusion of social media platforms if you're not grounded. The odds seem to be stacked against us. The distractions that our society have created only compound the difficulty in reaching inside to understand the true reasons we keep repeating the same mistakes over and over again. This is where Practicing LOVE helps to reestablish connections within ourselves and with each another.

Those of us who rely on social media to encompass our identity live within the void. It's a reason why we are able to scroll through social media watching videos or sharing pictures about babies being born, killings, crime, saving pets, bullying, and marriages within a two-minute span and be okay emotionally. Like nothing ever happened. Detached and disconnected. This happened so gradually over years that we didn't even know our brains were being re-wired. This is a systematic technique use by people in a position of power to indoctrinate their agendas upon a population. It's a psychological tool used to exploit our human needs: social validation and immediate gratification. The people creating these social media outlets tapped into those needs. And let's face it, it can be extremely addicting.

In 2013 the film *HER* gave us a glance of what's to come when it pertains to our identity and self-worth challenges. A gentleman who goes through a divorce has difficulty moving forward despite his attempt to date. He comes across an advertisement that features a new software that personalizes its responses according to yours and it evolves the more you interact with it. Soon it responded to his weaknesses and catered to his emotional needs of loneliness. It filled a void he couldn't find in others. He enters into an emotional relationship with the Artificial Intelligence (A.I.), and it's accepted by a co-worker who double dates with him and the voice of the A.I. Just three years later, in 2017, an app was developed to interact the same way. Amazed but not surprised, people who used the app have opened up more to the app than the developer could have imaged. You need to apply, answer many questions, and get accepted in order to receive a pass code to start. We retreat too easily from interactions into our safe house at the first sign of discomfort. We keep fueling the need for such A.I. to fulfill us instead of good old fashion human interaction, truth, and honesty.

Like any other addiction, an identity crisis arises. Society is filled with individuals who lack interpersonal skills, emotional intelligence and strength, or have difficulty standing strong on their own and facing challenges. Take school bullying as an example. It's gone from classroom harassment of passing notes to countless other social media avenues used to debase another person. Another effect is an increase in the suicide rate amongst teenagers. In 2017 the Center for Disease and Control reported an all-time high in the rate of teenage suicides. It's difficult to stand strong against anything when you have not yet discovered who you are. Loneliness embodies the heart and injects the mind into darkness.

Our senior citizens are neglected and left to fend for themselves without our assistance or love. Over the next twenty years, the population aged 65 and over is expected to grow from 48 million to 79 million. Meanwhile, the number of households headed by someone in that age group will increase by 66 percent to almost 50 million. By 2035 an astounding one out of three American households will be headed by someone aged 65 or older. The data are noted in the study, "Projections and Implications for Housing a Growing Population: Older Households 2015-2035" generated by the Joint Center for Housing Studies of Harvard University.

I've only briefly mentioned two topics around the bullying of teenagers and the neglect of our senior citizens. Both lead to people battling a crisis of loneliness.

This issue has become global. On January 28, 2018, United Kingdom's Prime Minister Theresa May appointed Tracey Grouch to a newly created position, Minister of Loneliness, to tackle the modern day problems associated with social isolation (NBC News). Yale University's Spring 2018 curriculum offered a new psychology course "Psychology and the Good Life" by Professor Laurie R. Santos. Twenty-five percent of its student body enrolled. A record breaking twelve hundred students. "In reality, a lot of us are anxious, stressed, unhappy, numb," Alannah Maynez, 19, a freshman taking the course said to a *New York Times* reporter (Published January 2018.) She and millions of others are in the same boat. After this semester, Yale will no longer offer the course. It stirred up problems between the professors and had unbalanced enrollment in the other courses. This course is not an anomaly. It was developed as a result of societal circumstances illustrating a real problem with our environment and its conditions.

The signs, facts, and proof that we are heading in a very dangerous direction are overwhelming. Our positive actions need to match the times if we are to survive as individuals and as a global society. We have to start relearning how to connect, how to express, and place love in the forefront of our core values, teachings, and consciousness. We will not survive as a society without love. Technology and power will always keep advancing. The two go hand in hand. Most people in a position of power do not operate from a place of love, which is why we are in this current state of crisis. We as a society have the power to turn this crisis around by empowering ourselves with knowledge and love. We can vote those in power out and elect those who have our best interest at heart. There is no excuse why we are unable to educate ourselves with the right information considering the advancement and access to technology. If we don't, there is no one to blame but ourselves. That is unacceptable in a country where we take our voting right for granted and have the power to create change. Another way to become proactive is to go into a field of study we wish to create change in and work from the inside out. We often wait too late to start. Usually after our children, family member, or friends have been killed by senseless gun violence or some other form of tragedy.

It is imperative that we act and start to change now before most of what we cherish and love diminishes with no way to rebuild or replenish. The connection we have with another will become unrecognizable.

Our current and future generations need grounding, self-awareness, and proper leadership. Practicing LOVE will assist in filling the void through human connectivity. In doing so we become more empathic and aware of the circumstances of over using social media tools.

FUTURE GENERATIONS

The advance pace of modern day living in conjunction with the various forms of artificial intelligence have created a battle ground for the fittest of families. Parents go to war trying to provide the best for their families while the cost of living continues to rise. The income level for blue-collar jobs remains the same, inflation continues, and benefits are stripped away slowly. Full-time employment has strategically been down-graded to part-time jobs in order to eliminate benefits. Walmart is an example of this business model. The Business Insider's Nandita Bose wrote the article, "Half of Walmart's Workforce are Part-Time Workers: Labor Group" (May 25, 2018). In this article she reports, part-time workers account for half of Walmart Inc's workforce, up from 20 percent in 2005, according to a labor group report on Friday that examined the company's increased shift away from more expensive full-time employees. Part-time employees receive fewer benefits, earn less pay for the same work as full-time associates and often find it hard to climb the ranks within the company. Fifty-five percent of part-time employees also said they did not have enough food to meet their basic needs. Walmart employees are among the largest groups on food stamp subsidies, according to labor experts.

Financial stress and survival factors build up within the family unit. For single parents, this pressure doubles. If we are occupied with more than one occupation to make ends meet, where does this leave our children? How much care and nurturing do they receive? From whom do they receive it? This leaves the gateway open for society to mold our children more than we are able to. This applies to all forms of family structures. We can never give enough care and love to children. We must not forget that children are the future and the foundation of all that stands on solid ground.

There was a time where most parents and elders looked after other children as their own with the same care and protection as given to their own families. In the past the love within the neighborhoods stemmed from one family to next. Some of us, like I remember, were taught to have respect for authority and elders. We may not have approved or liked all the adult figures in our lives, but the major difference now is the lack of respect for authority and elders. There are so many factors plaguing the minds of our youth causing them to have a major disconnect with adult figures and authority. Nowadays, we can watch YouTube videos of students launching to fight teachers; even young teenagers playing the knock-out game where they run up to stranger's: men, woman, and elders sucker-punching them unexpectedly and knocking them unconscious. We see children suing their parents, killing them, threatening and calling 911 at the heat of an argument. There is a sense of entitlement and narcissism that seems pandemic in this day and age that was not as prevalent as in the past.

In November of 2016, the United States census bureau released these statistics (release number CB16-192), "The second most common family arrangement is children living with a single mother, at 23 percent. These statistics come from the Census Bureau's Annual America's Families and Living Arrangements table package.

Between 1960 and 2016, the percentage of children living in families with two parents decreased from 88 to 69. Of those 50.7 million children living in families with two parents, 47.7 million live with two married parents and 3.0 million live with two unmarried parents.

During the 1960-2016 period, the percentage of children living with only their mother nearly tripled from 8 to 23 percent and the percentage of children living with only their father increased from 1 to 4 percent. The percentage of children not living with any parent increased slightly from 3 to 4 percent.

Households have grown smaller over time, reflecting the decrease in family size and the rise of living alone. The average number of people living in each household has declined from 3.3 people in 1960 to 2.5 today." The current financial times has caused a decrease in family size because raising a family is unaffordable.

One of the major factors leading up to the destruction of the family unit in causing a chain reaction of the facts listed above was the crack epidemic, which started in the 1980's. Crack cocaine literally destroyed households and lives like no other street drug. Minorities are always hit with the hardest forms of setbacks from educational cuts, fraudulent real estate loan practices, job opportunities, and drugs. The crack epidemic launched a mass incarceration and the start of multi-billion-dollar businesses of building and operating prisons. Laws were created and lengthened to keep people in prison longer giving no chance to restructure the family unit when people return to their homes. "From 1985 to 1992, city, state and federal legislators began to lengthen drug sentences. This was the heyday of the war on drugs. It included the Anti-Drug Abuse Act of 1986, which imposed even more mandatory minimum sentences. Most significantly, it set a five-year mandatory minimum sentence for offenses involving 100 grams of heroin, 500 grams of cocaine, or 5 grams of crack cocaine.

Two years later, new legislation added a five-year mandatory minimum sentence for simple possession of crack cocaine, with no evidence of intent to sell. Before then, one year of imprisonment had been the maximum federal penalty for possession of any amount of any drug (U.S. Department of Justice, Office of Justice Programs, *Bureau of Justice Statistics,* December 2016, NCJ 250229)." The incarceration level continues to rise even as the crime rate has gone down. Opioids have now become the dominating drug destroying family structure. There will always be a new drug unless we stop being consumers of it. Humanity is sounding the alarm giving us so many wake-up calls. We cannot afford to continue to sleepwalk through life. We need to rebuild our love for survival.

Another strange phenomenon that occurred within the past two decade is a shift in parenting methods, where the parent(s) wants to be their child's best friend instead of being a parent. How and why has modern day parenting evolved in this direction? Children need us to be all in as parents. They should choose their friends not have them imposed upon them. They need us to be strong when required and stern even when it hurts to be that way. That is our responsibility as parents. To do what's difficult under the most extreme situations all the while remaining focused and composed in setting an example. Our children will appreciate, thank us, and in some cases praise us when they have matured into adults and faced with similar experiences. It is at this point that we can develop the friendship aspect of the relationship with our children, not at teenage years. All these factors are informing us that we need to make changes soon before it is too late to restructure and build good old-fashioned family values.

Why is this information relevant? We now have all the stats and information we need to start making the necessary changes to rebuild our households and communities, re-structure the way we think, straighten out our core values, and become educated so we can make the system work in our favor rather than against us. We now understand the laws and systems put in place to oppress success with certain economical communities. We must force prisons to go out of business by staying out of them. We cannot afford not to be strong parents and deliver our absolute best so our children become amazing parents when their turn arrives.

Not only do we have to start Practicing LOVE, but we need to teach our children to practice love as well. By teaching our children to practice love, we reinforce values to improve our humanity. We decrease the chances of entitlement and narcissism from becoming their foundation. In cases where it already exists, Practicing LOVE will assist in cognitive restructuring and help instill healthier perspectives that ground one with humility, gratefulness, and humbleness.

We must not forget that children behave as mirror images. Our lives are examples for them. Their growth stems from the nurture of the love we give them. We also have to start viewing all children as our own and giving love when and where it's necessary. Children are the purest love we will ever know born into our world. We need to extend our hand and hearts to educate the core family values that have been lost. Love has the power to break cycles and establish and re-establish foundations. We have to be willing to give our all to ensure that our children survive with a healthy state of mind and achieve greatness. A good foundation with love develops amazing students and future leaders.

STUDENT & LEADERSHIP

We are in critical times where we need to develop our roles and become great students and great leaders. It has become difficult to view our public and political figures for leadership. Most of the agendas of those in power do not include love or function on love's behalf. Those that do are over powered by the majority that don't.

We have to allow ourselves to become a student at every opportunity that we can. As we become adults and obtain knowledge and experience, we sometimes forget that being a student of life is a lifelong role. We should always keep in mind and understand that we can learn those around us whether that person is an eight-year-old to an eighty-year-old. Viewing and listening to our youth will remind us of their fearlessness in taking chances, enabling adults to do the same. To bypass our fears and take calculated and thought out risks to achieve our goals. Listening is such a vital part of growing. I personally do more listening than talking. I usually speak if I have a point to make or contribute something constructive (keyword). If I'm just goofing around then it's a rap. It's difficult being quiet and not have diarrhea of the mouth. When we don't practice listening it becomes more difficult to do so. Not because we wish to speak but because we can't seem to quiet our minds and pay attention to details being discussed. Listening is the slightest form of mediation.

Here is an example of a life lesson I learned as an adult from a young lady. I recall viewing a story were a young girl's family went homeless while she was in grade school. By high school she was struggling and living with enormous stress. The key to her survival and success came out of her courage to ask for assistance and revealing her pain, exposing her vulnerability became her way out and a source of strength. The teachers chipped in all areas that required assistance. She graduated and attended college receiving a bachelor's degree. This young brave soul achieved what some of us think would be impossible. Training ourselves to be the best student in the most difficult circumstances. Educations is the key and way out for future generations. Her story gave me perspective and strength. It allowed me to understand the will to overcome any obstacles and achieve goals by being free of fear and the power of Practicing LOVE from others.

Our roles alternate back and forth depending on the situation. We then shift from student to leader. As adults, most of us will have families and need to set a great example for our children. In a household we take turns being leaders depending on the situation. The same may apply at work and in our surroundings, even with our friends. Someone may be getting into a situation that may end up with a negative outcome and circumstances, that's when we have to try and lead them into a positive direction. Before we become leaders of others, we will need to become leaders of ourselves by living the example we wish to see future children. Our leadership training also depends on the information we choose to fill our minds with and most importantly use our critical thinking process to determine what we choose to do with that information. Just because someone gives us information or we see in come from a media outlet doesn't mean we should not question it or check to see if it is correct by doing our own research. Becoming a critical thinker will limit the amount of times someone or entities will take advantage of us.

Our leadership skills will always need maintenance and up keeping. We have to keep our ego in check in times of leadership. It's easy for the ego to take over just because we are in a position of power. Empowerment also mean being in control and knowing when to cease power enabling us to grow and empower others to take their role in life. Practicing LOVE will allow us to maintain love in the forefront of our minds keeping our actions in check. It will also keep our visions clear allowing us to transition the two roles smoothly without selfish motives. Allowing this growth gains love, respect, and honor from others because we are giving it.

We can become a great leader in a fortune 500 company and still be grounded without letting our success get the better of us. Once we are in a position of power within any company then we have a responsibility to do what you can for others, from hiring, to developing scholarship, and mentorship opportunities so we can all benefit from the acts of Practicing LOVE. When we exercise our rights to achieve greatness, we will prevail.

JUDGING

On Tuesday, September 11, 2001 we were all struck with the same news of an unimaginable human catastrophe. Many lives were lost as we watched in shock and despair of what was taking place in front of our eyes. Not a common scene in America. We stood in disbelief of the invasion of our country by terrorists, an occurrence we believed only happened in other countries not ours. We were struck with the loss of life as we have never experienced before. We didn't know quite how to feel or react to such an act. Knowing American military history, it was just a matter of time before the attacks hit the United States. It was the first time in my life I witnessed individuals being violently mistreated and judged because others thought they might be culturally related to the terrorists.

I am not making an excuse for those who took part in this tragic act of violence. It's about opening our minds to understanding a bigger picture. If individuals were born into a culture where as a child a gun was placed in your hands and you were conditioned to hate with your heart, and your elders are setting these examples and living by them; most often than not, you will become one of them. This is their truth and reality. These individuals had no choice in how they were raised and conditioned. It is difficult to blame a person's action without truly understanding and knowing their history. We can't judge or define a culture, race, ethnicity based on the actions of a few individuals.

This type of conditioning occurs in our country every day. It's easy to look at an abusive parent and ask, "What kind of parent could do such a thing?" What if that parent was raised in an abusive home and made to understand that abuse is the meaning of love? Or, they could have been raised in foster homes that didn't foster love? We see individuals on drugs and automatically think it is by choice. We don't know if their mother had a substance abuse problem while pregnant causing direct harm to the fetus's brain and developing a chemical dependency while in the womb. We look at executives or companies, indulging in greed, who places profits at the expense of employees. What if the owner of the company was raised being rewarded with financial presents their whole lives instead of hugs, love, kisses, or simply being informed they did a great job? They were taught that the more money you obtain, the more successful you are replacing love with finance.

We are fast to place blame and point the finger. We are fast to cast the first stone without even processing the situation with all the evidence. It is so easy to jump on the band wagon than stand alone with your convictions. One of the easiest things to do is judge. This is one of the most difficult habits to break because of various issues blocking personal growth and keeping us from living in a healthy state of mind. When we judge, we dig deep inside ourselves and bring forth our negativity towards another; we are causing much harm to others as well as ourselves. We reinforce the negative emotions into our bodies and mind making it that much more difficult to practice the act of loving. We should never harm ourselves in such a manner—or others. We have to evolve and not judge on any level, especially the common ways in which we do judge others: appearance, color, race, styles, disabilities, height, occupation, and residencies.

It is not our place to judge others nor is it the right way to process life for a healthy outcome. Judgment is produced based on negative emotions triggered by processing others or a situation using our fears and ego to filter life. Most of the time we will never know all the facts behind unforeseen circumstances that occur in front of our eyes. The human spirit can only sustain so much before it breaks down, and the exterior elements take over despite of what is felt inside. Which is why we need to give away the love we generate whenever we can. To assist others and rejuvenate our own. We live in a country with an abundance of freedom and somehow we still choose to encase our minds and hearts from expansion and growth. The kind gestures that we practice will assist by transforming our internal core of viewing others without judgment. We will view people and situations for what they are instead of generating negativity and attaching it to individuals by letting our emotions get the best of us. We will then process life through a healthy and positive filter, allowing growth and love to lead the way.

PRACTICING GUIDELINES

Like experts in their respective fields, they became great with years of practice. Love works in a similar way. I am not saying that we will become experts in love. It will change our views and enhance our lives and those around us even those with whom we have brief encounters as we advance and move through life. This is about Practicing Love through one kind daily gesture that will evolve into a lifestyle and show others the power of love.

Practicing the act of love is difficult and by all means not easy at first. It gets better as time advances. Our intention has to be one of pure love not duty or obligation. In time it will be an automatic action like breathing. It will require some maintenance from time to time by grounding ourselves. That's because the world around us is hard at times and tears at us with many inhumane, cruel actions. A crowded train or bus can set us off in a negative spiral. Economic situations. Family disputes. We live in a culture that has political, financial, and educational designed to suppress the masses and increase our consumption with distractions and commerce.

The act of love requires us to learn how to start grounding ourselves if we haven't practiced this in other forms like meditation or yoga, connecting with nature, or simply enjoying quiet time to hear our inner voice without distractions. Questioning what we feel and think will start the exploration and forward momentum for a better understanding of who we are as an individual and as a whole in society.

The act of one kind gesture a day for over a year is the idea for this exercise. This is how we start to build and practice love. The act has to be pure in heart with zero expectations or even a thank you. Keep in mind that this exercise is for us not the individual(s) receiving it. If we find ourselves thinking quietly or out loud *I can't believe they didn't say thank you* or acknowledge me in any form then the gesture becomes impure and falls into negative energy. The action loses its strength, value, and purpose. Here again is where internal intent is important.

This also helps us develop patience so that our gestures become full of life. Lack of patience is one of the reasons we have a hard time understanding each other and ourselves. Rightfully so, we are extremely conditioned and addicted to instant gratification, a must-have attitude: I need it right now! A condition we need to break or minimize. Patience allows us to develop deeper, meaningful relationships whether at work or in our personal lives. We won't quit after our first big disagreement or fight. We work on understanding how to deal with each situation, how to understand our feelings, how to grow from each encounter. Patience will allow us to deal with the stresses life throws our way and keep life in perspective. It allows us to view our situation with a wider lens so we can adjust and pursue with confidence knowing we will overcome any obstacles. Patience takes time and the willingness to mature. There are no short cuts or apps to buy for this. Patience will teach us how to develop our social skills so we can see situations with clarity and make the right choices. It will allow us to grow in every aspect of our being.

Kind gestures can be anything like opening a door, giving a compliment, packing groceries or carrying them for a stranger, sending a thank you note, using your skills or talents to assist another, mentoring someone. Thank a co-worker for being thoughtful. If you're an artist, volunteer and face paint kids in hospitals or cancer treatment wards. Spend time helping or conversing with the elderly. If you're a business owner, give a product or service away to someone you feel is in need and can't afford it. Someone on the Internet posted a barber going into the streets and giving free haircuts to the homeless. It inspired other barbers to do the same. There are countless ways to give love. More often than not, people may look at you with a perplexed face and wonder or ask why you are thanking them. This allows us to inform them that we appreciate them and do not take the relationship or life for granted. We all need to be reminded and given love.

For example, I was on my way into the city feeling okay, nothing wrong although usually I'm a bit more cheery. I got in the elevator with a woman who walked in so delightfully, with an energy that changed my mood almost instantaneously. I had a huge smile on my face and said, "Good morning! Thank you so kindly for being delightful. It helped me." Her face lit up with surprise. I could see how much that meant to her in her eyes. She smiled and gestured like she was going to say something but didn't know quite what to say so I thanked her again as the elevator doors closed. It was an unexpected pleasant exchange. Sometimes that's all that's needed. She could have gotten great news that morning, who knows? What's important is that her demeanor, attitude, and energy made a difference. Her existence mattered. I am sure that knowing she made a difference to someone else by simply being herself made her feel even better.

Others who recognize the gesture of love will smile and say thank you, because they in turn give these gestures for similar reasons. This type of gesture sparks a chain reaction of thoughts in the receiver to pass it forward. This enhances all relationship and spreads the love. It's important to try and apply this in the work place as well since most spend on average eight hours a day at work. For many of us, our economy has forced us to have several jobs. This was not the case a few decades ago. A family could live on one salary. For freelancers and self-employed, any opportunity will apply. These small practices lead to bigger positive changes. Gestures are spontaneous and unpredictable like life. If the opportunity to practice love presents itself then we can move on them. If they don't then we offer ourselves and go out of our way to lend a hand.

Here is the kicker: For those who are addicted to social media, crave attention, compete to be liked, or need to be validated by others, these gestures of love cannot be boasted about or posted. They cannot be scripted or recorded. They cannot be pre-mediated. If we are truly sharing an experience to inspire the act of Practicing LOVE to another without selfish motives, then we are passing on our greatness to others. Deep down inside we will know the truth and if we are not honest it will backfire. We can choose to post our deeds, get a few likes and some feel good comments, pray it goes viral to make us feel like heroes, but it's fake and works against the very act we are trying to accomplish. In the end we are only cheating ourselves from the great gains this exercise has to offer.

We can keep track of these gestures in the journal. One of the requirements of Practicing LOVE is to journal. This will allow us to review the different gestures of kindness we are practicing. We can write about our daily gesture or about the experience with the receiver if there is one to record. There is no specific way of writing. We can express them through notes, stories, and drawings. If we have learned from an experience, express it in the journal. By journaling you will track it and help reinforce it into our memory, which can be used at a later time to pay it forward. This also makes us observant of kind gestures being done around us.

If we don't feel good emotionally or physically and are unable to perform one pure kind act that day, then don't. Let's save our energy for the following day. It's always better to give from the heart than perform a hollow gesture. We all have bad days. I suggest writing down what you were feeling that didn't allow you to perform the kind gesture. It's important to journal so we can release that energy and not carry it. Doing this allows us to see a pattern of behavior, potentially unhealthy behavior that we can address as well as our improvements and growth. If we are in the dumps and feel shitty, give physically not emotionally. It always makes me feel better. It's hard mustering up the strength to give when we are feeling this way. I am also aware that it's fine when I have nothing to give and need to be still. It allows for reflection. We can't give what we don't have. There will be times when we need to rejuvenate and replenish. We are human and vulnerable. However, if we let too much time go by without performing a deed, it will be like starting from scratch. Our momentum will lose strength, focus, and we will let daily life consume us with all the distractions. We need to remember that each day we wake up is a new day to start life fresh.

As weeks go by, we will be able to go back and see and feel the progress. We will be able to see what works or what doesn't work. This will allow us to move in the right direction. This will also bring kindness to the forefront and assist in structuring our life on a solid bedrock foundation. This will be the best gift we can give ourselves, and it will naturally spill into the lives of others. By the end of the year, we will understand and be able to see the bigger picture. This will be different for all who practice the act of love.

Several years ago, I was incredibly blessed that the world informed me of the outcome of one of my Practicing LOVE gestures. During my Barnes & Noble art tour in which I shared my art and read my poetry about my personal philosophy on life and love, a woman approached asking if I could speak to a friend of hers and share some of my words. I agreed. This friend and I meet in a conference room at the local library. I didn't know what to expect. I had never done anything like this. The gentleman spoke about his life and I gave some words of encouragement. I remember hugging him as he shed some tears. A short while later, the woman was moved by what happened and contacted me to help with a personal battle she was struggling with most of her life. It was an internal battle with her birth mother who didn't raise her. She struggled with abandonment and a sense of not being whole. Upon hearing further details, I informed her that she needed to find her mother; and forgive her if she had any chance of moving forward. I could clearly feel and see how this was eating her up inside. This forgiveness wasn't for her mother; it was for herself. She needed to start her healing process and begin to live a different stage in her life. She didn't want to inform her family about it. I agreed to help her find her mother and take her. Before long we had an address and went on a trip to her mother's house. As I pulled up, her tension and stress started to rise. I reassured her that no matter the outcome, she was going to start healing because she was doing everything in her power to move forward. I found a park where I waited and prayed before returning to the house to pick her up. Her energy was different. She looked settled with less tension. I didn't ask questions considering this was a super sensitive matter, and I didn't wish to stir anything up. I dropped her off and went about my life without further contact with her. A little more than a year had passed when I received a letter from this woman explaining the backstory of her life and the impact forgiving her mother had on her. I asked her permission to include the letter:

Dear Ray,

In order for you to understand my situation, I should have sent you this letter last year, but I needed to reflect and understand my unknowing circumstances taking place. I just wanted you to know that you have inspired, touched, and moved my life.

In the past, I was going through many difficult moments. In the insanity of my thoughts, I felt like I was a failure. I felt that I had accomplished nothing with my life knowing what I wanted. I did nothing to reach my goals and aspirations.

As a mother, I felt as if I did not encourage, teach, and love my children the way I wished. I felt like the worst mother in the entire world. I was unable to handle situations in my marriage. I failed to listen, share, and understand my partner. I tried to help others, but I felt that my efforts fell short. I wanted to do more but I just gave up.

I had stopped loving situations that used to bring joy to my life. I was experiencing something in my system that was very difficult for me to understand and explain. I wasn't happy no matter how hard I tried. I stopped believing in everything, including GOD. Many things kept adding on to my list of unhappiness, dislikes, and dissatisfaction. I got to a state of depression, bitterness, and loneness.

One day I got to the point I thought that there was no good reason for me to be here. I just did not want to belong any more. I had planned to commit suicide and finish what I thought at the moment was a worthless life. Without regrets or even thinking about how my decision would change the lives of the people I loved and looked at me as a role model; I just couldn't think straight.

Soon after, something happened about the same time I was going to end what I thought was a waste of space, my life. I put on my agenda that I was going to help someone. While I was finding a way to help that person, I saw you in Barnes & Noble near my neighborhood. We spoke about how you could help me help a person who I felt needed help. It soon became part of your agenda.

You were there to offer support and encouragement to that person when he needed it. I admired you because you devoted your time, expecting nothing in return. I witnessed the impact that you had made in that person's life and how you had opened a new world of possibilities for him. Then I began to think about my own situation. I thought how easy it was for you to make changes in his life through your literature, your art and by you just being you.

After browsing your web site, I felt I was able to feel love, the passion, and some of the pain in your art. I decided to have a brief conversation with you about the situation in my life regarding my mother. I recall after I finished mentioning my situation you said, "Look inside yourself. Find the forgiveness towards your mother and you will find that peace of mind that you have been looking for." You also said, "I needed to take care of myself, and sometimes I need to stop trying to be there for others when I can't be there for myself" or something like that. You told me that I needed to mentally prepared for whatever the outcome was going to be.

The intriguing part of this entire situation is that at that point you have no idea of the other reality; you had no clue of my unhappiness, bitterness or dissatisfaction in my life.

People say that GOD has his ways. I believe that you are a pure example of that. You had touched, inspired, and moved me in a way that no one had done before. You are blessed person. You have incredible charisma. GOD had put you in my path for a reason. I compare you with a guardian angel; you were there to encourage me in a very mysterious way.

I have to thank you for being there for me. Thanks for helping me in understanding that life is our most valuable belonging and without it we just cannot move on. Now I realize that I can be the best mother in the whole world and a better mother to my children. Now I understand that I have the power to change and manage situations in my life that had made me unhappy. Thank you because now I believe that GOD is there watching after me. Thank you for helping me in giving my life a second chance. Last December I had sent you a thank you card and wrote, "Thank you for giving back my life." I now hope you understand the full meaning of those words.

If you have to use my life situation/experience to help others to understand the meaning of life; what you do; or the meaning of your art, poetry or writings; and how you have touched my heart, please do.

Sincerely,

"Reflections from my past affecting my future"

It's been a while since I read her letter. As I reread it, I can't help but feel incredibly moved by her words and that experience again. It's as if I am reliving that moment and feeling those emotions all over.

Reading the letter that first time, I recall needing time to digest what I was feeling. I was overwhelmed and perplexed that someone would thank me or that I was part of helping in saving a life. Even the way it all unfolded was incredulous. How does one even start accepting that on any level? I had trouble with it for a while, because it was such a grand experience with all new emotions and feelings that I had never experienced before.

I came to realize that in order for me to be able to accept it I needed to place it back in her hands. After much contemplation, I gave her a call and informed her that I really didn't do much. She had the strength, courage, and desire inside her all along. She only needed a little assistance. Our exchange was very pleasant, and I felt as if part of my life was now connected with hers, that our energies intertwined leaving us connected until the end of time even if we never saw each other or spoke again.

She had given me as much as I had given her. It took me time to realize the magnitude of the exchange. She solidified and made me understand that the choice of following my inner voice to become an artist, and walk in faith was the right one. She helped give confirmation to my purpose, to the reason I decided to fight for humanity, to give my life to the work that I must do. I felt that if I had never painted or created again after understanding what I was a part of then it was all worth it. To help save one life or be part of the process. In the letter she mentioned she had nothing else to give before wanting to take her life. She mustarded up enough strength to ask for assistance to help another person. She did it without realizing that in return it would help save her life. An unmistakably true testimony to the power of giving and practicing love.

By Practicing LOVE we will never know who and how it will impact someone, how others will receive our love, and how it will return to us. It is one hundred percent true that we will never give without receiving in return when it comes to love. What we don't know is from who, how, or when we will receive it. These blessings usually come when we need it the most and the deliverer is unexpected. No form of Practicing LOVE will ever be too small. Each moment is powerful and will plant itself in the heart of the receiver to fulfill their call to life.

Another example of the impact of Practicing LOVE comes from Abigail Marsh, an Associate Professor in the Department of Psychology and the Interdisciplinary Neuroscience Program at Georgetown University. She received her PhD in Social Psychology from Harvard University in 2004 and conducted post-doctoral research at the National Institute of Mental Health until 2008. In June 2016, she was a guest speaker on TEDTalks. In her talk, she describes a life-altering experience she had at the age of nineteen: She was driving home one night on a freeway in Tokomak, Washington. A dog ran onto the freeway and she swerved to avoid hitting the dog sending her car into a fishtail spin across the freeway. When the car came to a halt, she was in the fast lane facing oncoming traffic—and the engine died. Fear encompassed her body as she was sure those were her last moments. Out of nowhere a gentleman ran across four lanes, started the car, got her to safety, and made sure she was okay to drive. He then got back into his car and drove off without ever giving his name. This act of love helped alter the course of Abigail's life. As a psychology researcher, she has dedicated her life studies to understanding the human capacity to care for others and the motivations of people who do extremely altruistic acts. Where does it come from? How does it develop? Why do some of us have it more than others?

What fires my heart's passion with love each and every time is seeing how the power of love evolves into the different stages of life and takes on a new form to move into the lives of others. To continue its journey restoring, giving hope, shining a new light, and stating I am alive and more powerful! I am LOVE. The example of love shared by Professor Abigail Marsh started when she was nineteen. We can't go back any further because the gentleman remains anonymous. Maybe someone saved his life? Maybe he saw a life being saved and that impacted him so much that it was then his turn to pass it on. We will never know when, why, and how this particular love started. In 2016, she shared that story on TEDTalks. In 2019, it was used as a comparative story to the Good Samaritan parable in a sermon by Rev. David Bisgrove. I happen to be sitting in one of the aisles listening. This loves journey will now continue in my book never knowing who will be impacted by the story of this particular love.

The results of Practicing LOVE are not always apparent, but they can be life altering. When we are gifted with knowing the impact, there is a powerful feeling that can fill our hearts with pure joy and a sense of purpose. Practicing LOVE became a part of my lifestyle. It has brought balance, more love and fulfillment to my life. It will continue to inspire and make a difference long after I am gone. This universal power of love we have will never diminish or be extinguished. When our physical state is no longer, the love we generated in our life time will be recycled into the veins and hearts of others who have partaken in our lives and be rejuvenated into another life force to continue its journey.

RESULTS

The results will be different for everyone. Within a couple of months of Practicing LOVE, we will fortify our lives and increase our drive to change. We will question our actions: Did I do the right thing? Am I doing what I can? Are my actions genuine? When we start to formulate our thinking and behavior through a positive stream of consciousness, we grow through love and reconnect with our spiritual self, with our true identity. We become less likely to go down the wrong track. Our vision is clear. We start seeing life through richer lenses and enjoy the simple things we come across every day. We share positive energy. Our temper subsides, and we learn to resolve situations through solutions based on kindness rather than spite or maliciousness because our ego was bruised. Empathy will live and thrive within us and restore our connection to one another.

Our choices will be concise and effective. Our choice to stand together and unite for a cause will be more powerful, because our actions will be derived from love. This will help us become better individuals, students, and leaders both at home and in our communities where the roots of our future foundation starts. We have a responsibility to honor the efforts of others from our past generations while ensuring the progression of our future ones. We need to help the next generation be in a better position than the present, from education to finance. Our present successes must leave our children with more tools and resources than we had. That's our responsibility.

We tend to look at others to see who is going to create the change that is needed when we each have the power to do so. We all need to be the best that we can to ourselves and those around us. We have to become strong so that our living situation and condition do not determine the outcome of our future—if we are in an unhealthy environment. Being grounded gives us the liberty and freedom to be critical thinkers. Not blindly accepting information presented to us as the absolute truth. We can do the research and educate ourselves to make intelligent choices. Once our actions based on anger are eliminated, we will no longer be controlled. This will help us make impactful societal choices, because we will see past the gimmicks of advertisements and propaganda. As critical thinkers, we will re-learn the truth about one's own history to prevent the same mistakes and build a better foundation so all can benefit from the power of love. As grounded freedom thinkers and doers, we can create the change in our life time not decades or centuries from now.

Our overall consumption of goods will lessen, because we will realize the unnecessary need to have more than necessary.

Over time, Practicing LOVE will restructure the way we view our past misfortunes when we embrace it with love. We will have healed, grown, and strengthened our character. We will understand what led to those circumstances in order to move forward, educate, and assist others who are experiencing similar situations.

We will have broken the cycle of repeating any negative behaviors our primary care givers have ingrained in us. We will change our environment if it is effecting us in a negative manner, because we have increased our value and understood our personal worth.

Past relationships (family/friendships/romantic) will be viewed as classrooms of life that allows us to graduate with greater knowledge about handling our future relationships so that we and others will benefit.

Practicing LOVE will open our minds and expand our visions on how to love and whom to love when the opportunity presents itself. We are stuck with high expectations of loving someone only if they meet 90 percent of our unrealistic criteria. That percentage will drop significantly because we will learn/relearn how to love with the real power developed from within not the exterior coating or the hollow romanticism created by society's unrealistic portrayal.

We will become better communicators. Communication is a key and vital component in all areas of our life. We will understand not to assume that others should know how we feel or believe they are mind readers. We will be grounded and in tune with ourselves. This will allow us to be clear and concise; communicating our emotions, feelings, intentions, views in life with one another without much miscommunication.

Our eyes will start to view others with a filter that connects humanity. We will judge less based on appearance, culture, situations, life style, financial status, and disabilities. I mention less because it's almost impossible not to slip and judge when we act on pure emotions without being in control. When we do, we will snap back into place and feel guilty or bad about having processed what occurred in that manner. We then realize we have to work harder to readjust and prevent that from reoccurring.

In addition, we learn to be true givers. Contributing to humanity truly only comes out of giving with pure and unselfish intensions. Once this becomes part of our life style, our mental and emotional health will improve. Less stress. Letting go of situations beyond our control and handling what we can control with grace and greatness.

It will assist in the intricacy of balancing our lives. Like the sun and moon both occupying the sky together yet allowing one another to take turns to fulfill their duty in balancing our universe for survival of all its inhabitants. Life will always require us to keep a balance which is why we need positive reinforcements like Practicing LOVE.

Doors will open to unexpected experiences, new friendships, job opportunities—even giving a stranger a reason to face another day. It builds courage, faith, self-resilience, focus, and the drive to make all things possible. This is the best of a win-win situation. It will help us be the person we envision and create the life we wish to live, a life with vibrancy, joy, accomplishments, and happiness. There will always be that constant internal battle to be free from the expectations of others. We will learn to define our choices based on our vision of happiness rather than on society's standards or someone else's projection of us. In the end if we are not in love with who we are and the way we are living, how can we possibly extend love to others?

As part of our growth and life lessons of Practicing LOVE, we will be tested to see if we are living what we have learned and gained through giving love with the purity of its intention. There will be times where we do not accomplish this with its full intent. It's not because we don't wish to or cannot, it's because we are conditioned to give love out of convenience not sacrifice. John Bunyan, an English writer born in 1628 says it best "You have not lived today until you have done something for someone who can never repay you." We will be tested in all the areas of our target growth. If we are working on patience, then it will be tested on all levels. If we are working on our identity, then all forms of distractions will pop up preventing us from working on ourselves. We have to be vigilant and aware in order to remain strong and focused on avoiding detours, setbacks, and traps. Once we become conscious of this factor, we will start to see the roadblocks and be able to avoid them. Remember, we are only human and it's inevitable that will slip and fall from time to time. The best part of this process is, as time passes and we continue to practice love, we bounce back from our falls even quicker with greater love to give. Being aware of this growth process will allow us to navigate life with confidence and assurance to live happier.

Happiness takes time to define and those answers usually come after we are comfortable with ourselves and know who we are. Life exchanges the good, the bad, the excitement of something great happening to us along with the heartfelt disappointments and anguish assist in discovering ourselves. Happiness is an internal growth that requires work like anything else. It's not going to magically appear especially with a cluster of issues plaguing our society and distractions. Time and patience will deliver happiness. As long as we work to better ourselves, it will come. It's also paramount to walk in faith and hope to live our outcome.

As a giver, I love doing just that, giving without wanting anything in return. I also needed to learn to receive as well; it's something I was not good at to say the least. I turned down someone willing to assist to me and learned a powerful—and humbling—lesson. It's not that I didn't want the assistance. I neglected to see it as part of the process. At some point, I realized that if I didn't accept from those who want to assist me with grace and humility, I would be denying them the very blessing of being able to give love away as I do with my life and art. This process is a two-way street, never one way. Receiving also rejuvenates our spirit and serves as fuel to keep us moving toward making a difference.

It's inevitable to get sidetracked or lose focus from time to time. Even now I experience it. Because I have been putting these principles in practice for years now, I've been able to quickly adjust and re-root myself. I won't lie to you. In the beginning it's difficult and takes many attempts. Here's an example to give you an idea regarding time, focus, and becoming conscious of putting small changes into practice on a daily basis. I have been saying "thank you" all my life as you probably have, too. It was part of the manners training from my parents. About two years ago, I wanted to introduce the word "kindly" at the end of my "thank you" as part of my daily gesture. Let's say when someone opened the door for me, I would reply "thank you kindly." It was a conscientious adjustment I wanted to make for no particular reason. It took me about 3 to 4 months until it became a natural part of my response. During that time, I would forget for days and sometimes a couple of weeks because I was reconditioning myself. The Practicing LOVE exercise is challenging and takes time. One of the ways I stayed focus and motivated was making sure I carried a notepad around all the time to document my progress. It supplied me with a physical item I could review as a reminder of what I needed to do. Hence, the reason for the journal section of this book. With all the love we start to give away, the journal helps to keep us on the right track. The journal helps us to stay focused on our newly developed roots and gives us a means to record our efforts and the outcomes.

Every new birth of a child is a miracle and a hope for humanity. That's what I visualize every time I see a pregnant woman. We are born with pure love in our hearts. Everything else is learned behavior. Give away your new grown love whenever possible and enjoy all the blessings life will offer. We should never take these gifts for granted. I could go on and on about the amazing outcomes I have experienced through Practicing LOVE, but this is where I stop and you start your amazing journey. It only gets more amazing as time goes on and we live by Practicing LOVE. Continue to read and absorb life as much as you can and never stop learning and growing. We should never be the same person from one year to another. We should always be evolving. I can tell you that the benefits of this exercise, Practicing LOVE, are limitless. The rest is up to you.

I look forward to living life through the filter of love with you. Many blessings and prayers.

Much LOVE,
ray

LOVE

1 Corinthians 13:4-7 New International Version

4 Love is patient, love is kind. It does not envy, it does not boast, it is not proud. 5 It does not dishonor others, it is not self-seeking, it is not easily angered, it keeps no record of wrongs. 6 Love does not delight in evil but rejoices with the truth. 7 It always protects, always trusts, always hopes, always perseveres.

These pages will allow you to journal about the topics discussed in the book. Be sure to date your entries in order to review your progress. In between are blank pages you can use them to sketch out your feelings or use it to collage your thoughts. You can add inspirational quotes, make a list of your future goals, personal objectives you wish to pursue, or a list of the people you wish to thank for their kindness or amends that need to take place.

_____

_____

_____

_____

_____

_____

_____

_____

_____

_____

_____

_____

_____

Photo by Julianny Casado